PROGRESS NOTES

Bible Study Guide for
Medical Students and Residents

To my students, past, present and future.

"Trust in the Lord with all your heart and lean not on your
own understanding.
In all your ways acknowledge him, and he will make your paths straight."

Proverbs 3:5-6

The problem every believing resident faces is how to exercise his spiritual muscles in order to live each day according to the priorities and values of his Christian faith within the challenging realities of internship. Besides an exponential amount of change, residents are dealing with ethical issues surrounding life and death. These issues are no longer abstract exercises of debate, but ones that directly impact the lives of their patients. Residents are challenged intellectually, ethically, and physically as they work long hours, eat irregular meals, deal with sleep deprivation and emotional isolation. Residency is a formative time professionally, and I believe spiritually as well.

This Bible study was originally created with interns in mind. The twelve Bible studies were designed to begin in July and occur monthly. The monthly topics were laid out in a sequence that addresses some of the many challenges faced by interns throughout the year. The Appendix contains twelve devotions, each one corresponding to the same topic as one of the studies. In between monthly meetings with a mentor or small group, the devotion could be sent electronically to the members of the small group or mentee in order to keep God's Word at the fore front of their minds.

Most interns need a lot of encouragement and flexibility in meeting. And as one of my wise students put it so candidly, "It is best to prepare for battle before you are in the midst of it." My prayer is that this set of Bible studies will be a useful tool for medical students and residents and those seeking to mentor them through these pivotal years.

You may contact me with suggestions or comments at

jane.goleman@osumc.edu

May God bless you and guide you each step of your journey.

Jane Goleman

Contents

Meeting #1: Expectations/Evaluations/Frustrations

Each year of medical education involves a significant increase in expectations and responsibilities. Internship may be the most physically and emotionally demanding year of residency. But whatever stage you find yourself in, consider what will be the most important and challenging aspects of the coming year. Comment on how you think you might be personally affected by these.

As medical students and residents, we are constantly being evaluated and receiving feedback about our performance. This can become a difficult way to live---under the pressure of continuous scrutiny. But on-going evaluation is a vital and necessary part of our training. We sometimes struggle with a sense of inferiority and incompetence, but on other days the pendulum swings and we experience success and a sense of accomplishment. These emotions are natural as we gain competence and learn from our experiences. The problem arises when the pendulum swings too far in one direction or the other. We can end up with a skewed view of our selves. We either ruminate about our inadequacies or relish grandiose thoughts of all our future accomplishments.

Sometimes it is not even the evaluation of others, but the expectations and demands we place on our selves that cause us the most distress. How can we remain grounded and have a healthy view of our selves and one another?

Read the following passage from **Romans 12:1-3** (The Message).

[1-2] So here's what I want you to do, God helping you: Take your everyday, ordinary life—your sleeping, eating, going-to-work, and walking-around life—and place it before God as an offering. Embracing what God does for you is the best thing you can do for him. Don't become so well-adjusted to your culture that you fit into it without even thinking. Instead, fix your attention on God. You'll be changed from the inside out. Readily recognize what he wants from you, and quickly respond to it. Unlike the culture around you, always dragging you down to its level of immaturity, God brings the best out of you, develops well-formed maturity in you.

[3]I'm speaking to you out of deep gratitude for all that God has given me, and especially as I have responsibilities in relation to you. Living then, as every one of you does, in pure grace, it's important that you not misinterpret yourselves as people who are bringing this goodness to God. No, God brings it all to you. The only accurate way to understand ourselves is by what God is and by what he does for us, not by what we are and what we do for him.

Read through the passage again, slowly. Look for the phrases that you find particularly relevant to your experience as a student or resident and mark them.

Questions for discussion:

1. How is "embracing what God does for you, the best thing you can do for him?"

2. How would you instruct someone to "fix his or her attention on God?

3. In verse one we are exhorted to place our lives before God as an offering, yet, in verse three we are warned not to misinterpret ourselves as the ones who are bringing this goodness to God. In what sense are we giving to God, and in what sense is God giving to us?

4. What does this passage say about how to accurately understand your self?

    Do you *really* believe that?

How do we usually go about understanding who we are and why we do things?

How would your life be different if you really believed that understanding who you are is based on what God is and what he does for you?

5. Consider how the truth of this passage can become a solid foundation for you, especially as you are evaluated and given feedback over the course of your training.

Pray: Take a few moments and pray, asking God to plant the truth you discussed in question 5 above deep into your life.

Set a tentative time for your next meeting.

Meeting #2: Clarifying Your Calling

As Christian physicians we each have our own perception about how we ended up as physicians. Some physicians describe *being called* by God to the practice of medicine. Other physicians say they *chose* medicine because it is an excellent way to serve God and others.

How would you describe the process in your own life?

Whatever your perception of *calling* and *choosing*, you are here now. You made it and you are practicing medicine. But, sometimes our present reality does not quite match what we imagined when we signed on. We tend to second guess our decisions when things don't go as expected. Having a strong sense of calling enables us to persevere when times get rough and external rewards drop off.

Os Guinness writes in *The Call,* "Our primary calling as followers of Christ is by him, to him, and for him. First and foremost we are called to Someone (God), not to something or somewhere. Our secondary callings (ie. our work and role in life) are our personal answer to God's summons."

Read the following verses from Ephesians and Philippians that speak to the subject of our calling.

Ephesians 2:8-10 (TNIV)

For it is by grace you have been saved, through faith---and this not from yourselves, it is the gift of God—not by works, so that no one can boast. For we are God's handiwork, created in Christ Jesus to do good works, which God prepared in advance for us to do.

Ephesians 4: 1-3 (TNIV)
As a prisoner for the Lord, then, I urge you to live a life worthy of the calling you have received. [2] Be completely humble and gentle; be patient, bearing with one another in love. [3] Make every effort to keep the unity of the Spirit through the bond of peace.

Philippians 2:12-13 (TNIV)
Therefore, my dear friends, as you have always obeyed---not only in my presence, but now much more in my absence---continue to work out your salvation in fear and trembling, for it is God who works in you to will and to act according to his good purpose.

Questions for discussion:

1. In Ephesians 2:8-10 'works' is repeated several times. List all the different kinds of work God has done. Then, put these verses into your own words.

2. Have all Christians received a calling?

3. What does a life worthy of God's calling look like? How might we be in danger of living below our calling?

4. In Philippians 2:12-13, what does it mean "to work out your salvation"?

    Why with fear and trembling?

5. In Philippians we see the word 'work' repeated again. What is God's work and what is our work?

God works in us to prompt us to pursue our calling, which is our response to his salvation and presence in our lives. For some, our calling remains the same throughout our lives, but for most, we continue to grow into our calling as we continue to mature in our faith.

6. How would you define your calling right now as a student or resident?

Black Box Warning:
1. Everyone seems to have a plan for our lives! We must develop a deep relationship with God that makes his voice familiar enough to be recognized over the noise of other voices calling out instructions and plans for us.

2. When our emotional energy gets low, it makes it difficult to hear God. If you feel burned out right now, you're probably feeling numb to almost everything. Before making any important decisions about the direction of your life, you need to take time to rest and renew your physical and emotional energy.

It doesn't take a person with awesome skills or even spiritual maturity to be used by God. What it takes is a person who is willing to be used, who says, "Lord, I'm available to You. Use me as You want."

We are all in different places when it comes to working out our calling. Even if we have been _called_ to medicine, we must continue to discern what kind of medicine we will practice, with whom? for whom? where? It is an on-going process and proceeds best in prayer.

Pray: Use the following prayer and have one person open and one person close.

Open: Father God, we humble ourselves before you in gratitude for all the work you have done for us and are doing in us. We choose to take our eyes off of our selves, off of "our calling" and onto the One who calls. Thank you for calling us to your self.

Conversational prayer:

Close: You are holy, holy, holy. You are worthy of our worship---all that we are and have. Empower us with your Spirit that our work, our words, and our hearts would bring you honor. Sustain us with your Spirit. Teach us to rest in You, even as we work. Give us ears to hear your voice over all others.
In Jesus' name. Amen

Choose one Scripture verse to meditate on over the next week:
For the eyes of the Lord search back and forth across the whole earth, looking for people whose hearts are perfect toward him, so that he can show his great power in helping them. 2 Chronicles 16:9

This is what the Lord says, he who made the earth, the Lord who formed it and established it----the Lord is his name: "Call to me and I will answer you and tell you great and unsearchable things you do not know." Jeremiah 33:2-3

I will instruct you and teach you in the way you should go: I will counsel you and watch over you. Psalm 32:8

Always give yourselves fully to the work of the Lord, because you know that your labor in the Lord is not in vain. I Corinthians 15:58

Seek first his kingdom and his righteousness, and all these things will be given to you as well. Matthew 6:33

Delight your self in the Lord and he will give you the desires of your heart. Psalm 37:4

Other resources for further reading:

Guinness, Os. *The Call: Finding and Fulfilling the Central Purpose of Your Life*. Nashville, TN: Word Publishing, 1998.

Peel, Bill and Kathy. *Discover Your Destiny: Finding the Courage to Follow Your Dreams*. Colorado Springs, CO: NavPress, 1996.

Willard, Dallas. *Hearing God: Developing a Conversational Relationship with God*. Downers Grove, IL: InterVarsity Press, 1999.

Meeting #3: Burden of Caring with Integrity

It is easy to become "weary in doing good." (Galations 6:9) Granted that physical and emotional exhaustion may accelerate that weariness! But Galatians encourages us, "Let us not become weary in doing good, for at the proper time we will reap a harvest if we do not give up."

When we are chronically fatigued our default mode may become one of irritability and grumpiness disintegrating quickly to cynicism. As one intern put it, "I found myself 'throwing fits in my head,' when answering 'stupid' pages from nursing staff." Often we continue to do our job (or "to do good"), but it is with an attitude. We can become snarly! I wonder if that is how the disciples were feeling late in the day when they were tired and hungry and wanting some down time. They had just returned from their first ministry trip and were eager to get some time with Jesus and fill him in on all they had seen and done.

Luke 9:10-17 (TNIV)

[10-11]The apostles returned and reported on what they had done. Jesus took them away, off by themselves, near the town called Bethsaida. But the crowds got wind of it and followed. Jesus graciously welcomed them and talked to them about the kingdom of God. Those who needed healing, he healed.

[12]As the day declined, the Twelve said, "Dismiss the crowd so they can go to the farms or villages around here and get a room for the night and a bite to eat. We're out in the middle of nowhere."

[13-14]"You feed them," Jesus said.

They said, "We couldn't scrape up more than five loaves of bread and a couple of fish—unless, of course, you want us to go to town ourselves and buy food for everybody." (There were more than five thousand people in the crowd.)

[14-17]But he went ahead and directed his disciples, "Sit them down in groups of about fifty." They did what he said, and soon had everyone seated. He took the five loaves and two fish, lifted his face to heaven in prayer, blessed, broke, and gave the bread and fish to the disciples to hand out to the crowd. After the people had all eaten their fill, twelve baskets of leftovers were gathered up.

Read the passage again slowly. Notice Jesus' attitude toward the people.

Questions for Discussion:

1. Why do you think people's physical needs were part of Jesus' ministry?

2. What has been your experience in meeting people's physical needs in terms of ministry?

3. When have you felt overwhelmed by people's physical needs? How did you handle it?

4. What all did the disciples need to learn before Christ could use them in feeding the crowd?

   Are there similar lessons we need to learn in order for Christ to use us to meet the needs of others?

5. Notice how Jesus begins by organizing the crowd. When you are feeling overwhelmed in meeting people's needs is there a way you might use this principle? (How do you eat an elephant? One bite at a time!)

As physicians we have the ability to get things done, to solve problems, to just work harder until we figure out a way. But sometimes our strength in our abilities can become our greatest disability. We need to take our cue from Christ who said, "I do nothing on my own but speak just what the Father has taught me" (John 8:28). In John 12:49, Jesus said, "For I did not speak of my own accord, but the Father who sent me commanded me what to say and how to say it." Even *how* to say it! We need to live our days in constant awareness of Christ, and submission to his will and his way. Our greatness lies in our surrender to God.

Discuss any practical ways you can increase your awareness and dependency on Christ throughout your day. Are there any physical reminders you might incorporate into your routine?

Spend some time in prayer following the "ACTS" mnemonic:

Adoration:

Confession:

Thanksgiving:

Supplication:

"No one is stronger than the weakest person who is totally dependent on God."   Roy Lessin

Meeting #4: Finding Meaning in the Mundane: Relentless Scut-Work

How to drive an intern crazy? Chronic sleep deprivation, erratic meals, emotional isolation, and no control over his/her schedule. Then add in relentless and seemingly meaningless tasks. AAUUUGGGHHHH ! ! !

We can be thankful that internship does not last a life time!!! But it is a season. . . an unforgettable season of training. How can we take the angst of medical school and residency and leverage it for our spiritual growth? Instead or growing more jaded and cynical, how can we preserve our ideals and actually become more like Christ?

Take a moment to reflect on one or two attributes or ideals that are important to you and which you believe are connected with the process of becoming a physician. Describe an experience that has made this connection even more significant for you.

Hebrews 12 encourages us to endure hardship and to allow it to train us in righteousness and peace. When we consider the cloud of witnesses the author of Hebrews refers to in chapter 11, along with many contemporary believers who are being persecuted for their faith in other parts of the world, our struggles and irritations may seem petty. That being said, we can still gain principles and truth from this text to encourage and enable us to persevere and grow during tough times.

Hebrews 12 (TNIV)

[1] Therefore, since we are surrounded by such a great cloud of witnesses, let us throw off everything that hinders and the sin that so easily entangles. And let us run with perseverance the race marked out for us, [2] fixing our eyes on Jesus, the pioneer and perfecter of faith. For the joy set before him he endured the cross, scorning its shame, and sat down at the right hand of the throne of God. [3] Consider him who endured such opposition from sinners, so that you will not grow weary and lose heart.
[4] In your struggle against sin, you have not yet resisted to the point of shedding your blood. [5] And have you completely forgotten this word of encouragement that addresses you as children? It says,

> "My son, do not make light of the Lord's discipline,
> and do not lose heart when he rebukes you,
> [6] because the Lord disciplines those he loves,
> and he chastens everyone he accepts as his child."

[7] Endure hardship as discipline; God is treating you as his children. For what children are not disciplined by their father? [8] If you are not disciplined—and everyone undergoes discipline—then you are not legitimate children at all. [9] Moreover, we have all had parents who disciplined us and we respected them for it. How much more should we submit to the Father of spirits and live! [10] Our parents disciplined us for a little while as they thought best; but God disciplines us for our good, that we may share in his holiness. [11] No discipline seems pleasant at the time, but painful. Later on, however, it produces a harvest of righteousness and peace for those who have been trained by it. [12] Therefore, strengthen your feeble arms and weak knees. [13] "Make level paths for your feet," so that the lame may not be disabled, but rather healed.

Questions for Discussion:

1. How would you describe the race set out for you? (a jog by the lake, uphill all the way, a marathon in a torrential downpour . .)

2. Name two obstacles that have been hindering and entangling you recently as you run. (Why is it that sin *so easily* entangles us?)

3. How might "considering Jesus" help you endure?

4. Have you discovered any practical things that help you keep your eyes fixed on Jesus?

5. Verse seven says, "Endure hardship as discipline." What redeems hardship from just being plain old hard, and makes it a discipline that leads to holiness in Christ?

6. Brainstorm about the kind of rehab or physical therapy you would recommend for your feeble arms and weak knees.

    Is there any way to make your path more manageable? (realizing you don't have much control over your schedule, what do you have control over?)

Pray: Spend some time together in prayer, fixing your eyes on Christ. Follow the ACTS mnemonic, and go back and forth through each.

Adoration:

Confession:

Thanksgiving:

Supplication:

Name one truth you want to remember from this lesson and one action you want to take.

Meeting #5: Delayed Gratification and a Sense of Entitlement

The life of a medical student or resident is a life of delayed gratification. So much of life seems to be put on hold, whether it is buying a home, having a baby, or singing on the worship team. Delayed gratification has the potential to develop self discipline and to lead to a deeper sense of appreciation, BUT on the flip side, it can develop into bitterness, resentment, and a warped sense of entitlement.

Entitlement refers to someone's belief that he or she is deserving of some particular reward or benefit. It is often used as a negative term of an exaggerated or rigidly held sense of entitlement. The combination of delayed gratification and a sense of entitlement set the scene for a BIG FALL.

Immediate gratification is one of Satan's most successful lures to temptation. We are unapologetically addicted to the immediate; we feel justifiably discontent with delay. Why should we wait when it is in our power not to? Many a student or resident has fallen prey to this line of thinking - - - hook, line, and sinker !

Physicians have the power to spend money. Even if we are in major debt, we can easily qualify for credit cards, loans, and mortgages. And buying new things has a way of making us feel better. It lifts our spirits. It's a fix - - - at least temporarily. Besides we have certainly worked hard enough. Why wait to get the new car or latest TV? You deserve it. You are a physician and you need to start living like one!

Delayed gratification plus a sense of entitlement, plus the ability, equals DANGER ! Physicians have a lot of ability: the ability to spend, to acquire drugs, to exploit others emotionally or sexually, etc. Physicians have the power and opportunity to feed their appetites. Appetite is our most basic layer of vulnerability when it comes to temptation. No amount of education or height of accomplishment can substitute for self-control when it comes to our appetite.

READ Luke 4:1-13

[1] Jesus, full of the Holy Spirit, left the Jordan and was led by the Spirit into the wilderness, [2] where for forty days he was tempted by the devil. He ate nothing during those days, and at the end of them he was hungry.

[3] The devil said to him, "If you are the Son of God, tell this stone to become bread."

[4] Jesus answered, "It is written: 'People do not live on bread alone.' "

[5] The devil led him up to a high place and showed him in an instant all the kingdoms of the world. [6] And he said to him, "I will give you all their authority

and splendor; it has been given to me, and I can give it to anyone I want to. [7] If you worship me, it will all be yours."

[8] Jesus answered, "It is written: 'Worship the Lord your God and serve him only.' "

[9] The devil led him to Jerusalem and had him stand on the highest point of the temple. "If you are the Son of God," he said, "throw yourself down from here. [10] For it is written:

" 'He will command his angels concerning you
   to guard you carefully;
[11] they will lift you up in their hands,
   so that you will not strike your foot against a stone.' "

[12] Jesus answered, "It is said: 'Do not put the Lord your God to the test.' "

[13] When the devil had finished all this tempting, he left him until an opportune time.

Questions for Discussion:

1. Consider all the ways your medical training compares with Jesus in the wilderness (vv.1-2). Consider also the timing in relationship to his career.

2. In each temptation, what was its appeal? Its price? How does Jesus resist?

   a.) stone to bread

   b.) authority of all the kingdoms of the earth

   c.) jump off the Jerusalem temple so the angels will catch you

3. Author, Alicia Britt Chole identifies these three temptations as the lure of appetite, authority, and applause. How are these lures relevant to students and residents?

4. Under what circumstances are you most susceptible to temptation?

> It is when we forget who we are that we are most vulnerable to bowing down. Personally, I think Satan's real hope was that Jesus would somehow---because of the heat or the hunger or the loneliness or the sheer dazzle of the world and its splendor---lose sight of eternity even for a moment and forget who he really was.[1]
> *Alicia Britt Chole*

5. How are the three temptations similar?

> Only one true temptation in our spiritual lives: to choose against God.[2]
> *Alicia Britt Chole*

6. How can you recognize temptation for what it is?

7. If the tempter had three shots at you, what three temptations would he use?

8. What can help you resist?

> Temptation twists truth. The longer we wait to reposition our appetite behind God's will and word, the fuzzier truth becomes in our brains. Look away from the lure and towards God's word.[3]
> *Alicia Britt Chole*

---

[1] Alicia Britt Chole, *Anonymous* (Franklin, TN: Integrity Publishers, 2006) 144.

[2] Ibid. 167.

[3] Ibid. 88.

Close with Prayer:

Consider what was shared during this meeting together and pray for each other against giving in to temptation.

Meeting #6: Connecting with God

"Jesus never taught His disciples how to preach, only how to pray."
                                                                Andrew Murray

As students and residents, prayer is the one spiritual discipline that we practice the most, even if it is brief and urgent - - - "Help Lord!"   Difficult circumstances can press us closer to God. Our prayers will be more effective when we keep in mind who we are praying to. When we remember who God is our faith increases, and we can pray in faith believing that he hears us and will answer our prayers.

"Have faith in God," Jesus answered. . . . "Whatever you ask for in prayer, believe that you have received it, and it will be yours."   Mark 11:22, 24

"Have faith in God." This faith (faith in God) precedes the faith *in the promise* of an answer to prayer.

 "The power to believe a promise depends entirely on faith in the promiser."
                                                                Andrew Murray

So often we concentrate on a certain promise in Scripture claiming it for ourselves in faith. But when it never seems to come about we are ready to give up. The promise is true, but our faith is lacking. We must direct our faith toward God, then we will have faith to grasp his promises. Many residents have found the Psalms helpful during stressful times. Certainly David's faith in God and heartfelt honesty can serve us well as we try to put our "angst" into prayers to God.

In a remarkable way, Psalm 51 reveals the true nature of sin as a broken relationship with God. The psalm takes us through the stages of repentance. It describes the rumination, the gnawing guilt, the shame, and finally the hope of a new beginning that comes from true repentance.

Psalm 51: 1-12 (TNIV)

For the director of music. A psalm of David. When the prophet Nathan came to him after David had committed adultery with Bathsheba.

[1] Have mercy on me, O God,
   according to your unfailing love;
   according to your great compassion
   blot out my transgressions.

[2] Wash away all my iniquity
   and cleanse me from my sin.

[3] For I know my transgressions,
   and my sin is always before me.

[4] Against you, you only, have I sinned
   and done what is evil in your sight;
   so you are right in your verdict
   and justified when you judge.

[5] Surely I was sinful at birth,
   sinful from the time my mother conceived me.

[6] Yet you desired faithfulness even in the womb;
   you taught me wisdom in that secret place.

[7] Cleanse me with hyssop, and I will be clean;
   wash me, and I will be whiter than snow.

[8] Let me hear joy and gladness;
   let the bones you have crushed rejoice.

[9] Hide your face from my sins
   and blot out all my iniquity.

[10] Create in me a pure heart, O God,
   and renew a steadfast spirit within me.

[11] Do not cast me from your presence
   or take your Holy Spirit from me.

[12] Restore to me the joy of your salvation
   and grant me a willing spirit, to sustain me.

Questions for Discussion:

1. In light of David's arrogance, adultery, deception and murder, how does David dare approach God? What does he feel? Who does David believe God to be?

2. What may we learn about confession and the grounds of forgiveness from verses 1-5?

3. David realizes that his whole nature is sinful, and that God requires sincerity and integrity in the innermost part of his being. What, therefore, (in verses 7-12) does he ask for in addition to forgiveness?

4. Has covering up sin backfired in your life? How have you seen God's mercy when you owned up to your sin?

5. Write out verses 10 -12 in your own words---your own request to God.

Never disregard a conviction that the Holy Spirit brings to you. If it is important enough for the Spirit of God to bring it to your mind, it is the very thing He is detecting in you. You were looking for some big thing to give up, while God is telling you of some tiny thing that must go.

But behind that tiny thing lies the stronghold of obstinacy, and you say, "I will not give up my right to myself"— the very thing that God intends you to give up if you are to be a disciple of Jesus Christ.

Oswald Chambers

Prayer Time:

Anything that hinders our relationship with God will hinder our communication with God and his answers to prayer, whether it is our lack of faith in God or sin in our life. In the ACTS mnemonic for prayer: **A**doration reminds us of who God is and **C**onfession clears the way for unbroken communication.

Use the ACTS mnemonic to spend some time in prayer together right now. Pray **Adoration** together and then have a silent prayer of **Confession**. Designate who will break the silence with **Thanksgiving,** and then both pray your prayers of **Supplication** from your answer to question 5 above.

The sacrifices of God are a broken spirit, a broken and a contrite heart, O God, you will not despise   Psalm 51:17

Where to Get Help in the Book of Psalms

When you feel . . .

Afraid 3, 4, 27, 46, 49, 56, 91, 118
Alone 9, 10, 12, 13, 27, 40, 43
Burned Out 6, 63
Cheated 41
Confused 10, 12, 73
Depressed 27, 34, 42, 43, 88, 143
Distressed 13, 25, 31, 40, 107
Elated 19, 96
Guilty 19, 32, 38, 51
Hateful 11
Impatient 13, 27, 37, 40
Insecure 3, 5, 12, 91
Insulted 41, 70
Jealous 37
Like Quitting 29, 43, 145
Lost 23, 139

Overwhelmed 25, 69, 142
Penitent/Sorry 32, 51, 66
Proud 13, 30, 49
Purposeless 14, 25, 39, 49, 90
Sad 13
Self-confident 24
Tense 4
Thankful 118, 136, 138
Threatened 3, 11, 17
Tired/Weak 6, 13, 18, 28, 40, 86
Trapped 7, 17, 42, 88, 142
Unimportant 8, 90, 139
Vengeful 3, 7, 109
Worried 37
Worshipful 8, 19, 27, 29, 150

When you want . . .

Acceptance 139
Answers 4, 7
Confidence 46, 71
Courage 11, 42
Fellowship with God 5, 16, 25, 27, 133
Forgiveness 32, 38, 40, 51, 69, 86,103
Friendship 16
Godliness 15, 25
Guidance 1, 5, 15, 19, 25, 32, 48
Healing 6, 41
Hope 16-18, 23, 27
Humility 19, 147
Illumination 19
Integrity 24, 25
Joy 9, 16, 28, 126

Justice 2, 14, 26, 37, 49, 58, 82
Knowledge 8, 19, 25, 29, 97,103
Leadership 72
Miracles 60, 111
Money 15, 16, 17, 49
Peace 3, 4
Perspective 2, 11
Prayer 5, 17, 27, 61
Protection 3, 4, 7, 16-18, 23, 27, 31, 91, 121, 125
Provision 23
Rest 23, 27
Salvation 26, 37, 49, 126
Stability 11, 33, 46
Vindication 9, 14, 28, 35,109
Wisdom 1, 16, 19, 64, 111

Meeting #7: Refuse to Be Offended

The last meeting was about prayer and how the power to believe a *promise* depends entirely on faith in the *promiser*. Trust in the person produces trust in what he says. In prayer everything depends on the clarity of our relationship with God

In Mark 11:22-24, Jesus exhorts his disciples to "Have faith in God," . . . and that "whatever you ask for in prayer, believe that you have received it, and it will be yours." And in the very next verse, Mark 11:25, Jesus says, "And when you stand praying, if you hold anything against anyone, forgive them, so that your Father in heaven may forgive you your sins." This same principle is repeated in the Lord's Prayer: "And forgive us our debts as we also have forgiven our debtors." (Matthew 6:12) It seems for our prayers to be effective, our relationships with other people must also be clear.

Love of God and love of our neighbor are inseparable.

[20-21]If anyone boasts, "I love God," and goes right on hating his brother or sister, thinking nothing of it, he is a liar. If he won't love the person he can see, how can he love the God he can't see? The command we have from Christ is blunt: Loving God includes loving people. You've got to love both. (1 John 4:20-21 The Message)

The prayer from a heart that is not right with God or with other people will not succeed. This study focuses on our relationships with others- - - more specifically, having a forgiving spirit. We often think of forgiveness when it comes to something BIG, like betraying a confidence, or committing adultery. But what about the little things - - -the daily things? This is the training ground in which our habits take root and our character is forged.

It is the daily irritation that can steal our joy and distract us from God's agenda. We may not even realize it as an issue of forgiveness. As a resident there are so many opportunities to take offense. Any many *do* seem justified. Take the call schedule for example . . .

Questions for Discussion:

1. Discuss where you draw the line between not wanting to be taken advantage of and just forgiving the other person, or letting go of a situation. Give a recent example from your own life.

2. Is it possible to choose *not* to take offense and still work to remedy an unjust situation? Can you give an example?

3. Take a moment and ask God to give you fresh insight into this familiar passage on love and to learn things you haven't before. Then **read this passage** from 1 Corinthians 13:3b-7 (The Message).

No matter what I say, what I believe, and what I do, I'm bankrupt without love.

Love never gives up.

Love cares more for others than for self.

Love doesn't want what it doesn't have.

Love doesn't strut,

Doesn't have a swelled head,

Doesn't force itself on others,

Isn't always "me first,"

Doesn't fly off the handle,

Doesn't keep score of the sins of others,

Doesn't revel when others grovel,

Takes pleasure in the flowering of truth,

Puts up with anything,

Trusts God always,

Always looks for the best,

Never looks back,

But keeps going to the end.

4. Paul is writing in response to the Corinthians' quest for power and spiritual gifts,   when he says, "No matter what I say, what I believe, and what I do, I'm bankrupt without love." As students or residents our quest may be for control, power, accolades, or just to get out of the hospital early for once. What are you in danger of saying, or believing, or doing that becomes an obstacle to really loving others?

5. Opposite each description of love in the passage above, try to write a one-word summary. Which of these qualities have you experienced in your relationship with God?

6. What does it take to avoid "taking things personally"? And why *not* take things personally when they were *meant* to be personal? What do we gain by being offended? What do we lose?

7. *"A tendency toward perfectionism, can work against a spirit of forgiveness, whether it is in relation to forgiving our selves or those who work with us."*

Do you agree or disagree, and why?

[18-20]My dear children, let's not just talk about love; let's practice real love. This is the only way we'll know we're living truly, living in God's reality. It's also the way to shut down debilitating self-criticism, even when there is something to it. For God is greater than our worried hearts and knows more about us than we do ourselves.   I John 3:18-23 (The Message)

The spirit of forgiveness is the spirit of love. Because God is love, He forgives. It is only when we are dwelling in love that we can forgive as God forgives.

8. So, the next time you are feeling offended whether it is from being slighted by a friend or the motor vehicle now in front of you, remember you have a choice. It is difficult to make the choice NOT to be offended if we don't prepare ahead of time for that option. What might you do that would enable you to choose not to be offended?

Wouldn't these words make great advice for how to survive internship and residency?

The best residents never give up. They care more for others than themselves. They don't want what they don't have. They don't strut and have big heads. They don't force themselves on others, or always put themselves first. The best residents don't fly off the handle, or keep score of wrongs done to them. They don't revel when others grovel, but they take pleasure in the truth. They put up with anything. The best residents trust God always, look for the best, never look back and keep going to the end!

Close with prayer:

Adoration: Recount the ways God has shown his love to you.

Confession: Confess where you have fallen short of a forgiving nature in your daily life.

Thanksgiving: Praise God for his forgiveness and ability to change you into his likeness. That it isn't about us, but all about Him.

Supplication: Ask God to teach you how to love and forgive, and to point out the weaknesses in your relationships with others that might hinder your fellowship with him.

Meeting #8: Burnout

"All his days his work is pain and grief; even at night his mind does not rest. This too is meaningless." Ecclesiastes 2:18

Identify a negative or disappointing clinical or work-related experience (such as a medical mistake, critically ill or dying patient, professional conflict, or negative feedback on your performance) that has occurred recently. What was your reaction to this experience? Did any positive changes occur from this experience? If so, describe them.

Burnout is a syndrome of depersonalization, emotional exhaustion, and a sense of low personal accomplishment that leads to decreased effectiveness at work.[4] Many, many residents and physicians experience burnout. The sequence of factors begins with emotional exhaustion, then depersonalization in relationships with co-workers, then a sense of inadequacy or reduced personal accomplishment.

---

[4] Maslach C, Jackson SE, Leiter MP, *Maslach Burnout Inventory Manual*. 3rd ed. (Palo Alto, CA: Consulting Psychologists Pr., 1996).

Perhaps the Old Testament prophet Elijah's experience is somewhat similar to burnout. Elijah was a ninth century B.C. prophet who stood for God in one of the darkest chapters of Israel's history (1 Kings 17:1-19:21) Elijah covered a lot of ground during his ministry as he traveled back and forth in his home territory of Gilead, which is a mountainous region on the eastern shore of the Jordan river.

Elijah's defeat of 850 false prophets on the top of Mt. Carmel is described in 1 Kings 18:16-40. After this spiritual show down between Baal and the God of Israel, Elijah had the false prophets slaughtered in the Kishon Valley. He then climbed back up the mountain and prayed for rain. Then he ran sixteen miles to Jezreel. From Jezreel to Beersheba (in 1 Kings 19:4) is ninety miles. From Beersheba to the wilderness of Judah is another twenty miles. No wonder he was exhausted physically and emotionally.

Read 1 Kings 19

1-2 Ahab reported to Jezebel everything that Elijah had done, including the massacre of the prophets. Jezebel immediately sent a messenger to Elijah with her threat: "The gods will get you for this and I'll get even with you! By this time tomorrow you'll be as dead as any one of those prophets."

3-5 When Elijah saw how things were, he ran for dear life to Beersheba, far in the south of Judah. He left his young servant there and then went on into the desert another day's journey. He came to a lone broom bush and collapsed in its shade, wanting in the worst way to be done with it all—to just die: "Enough of this, GOD! Take my life—I'm ready to join my ancestors in the grave!" Exhausted, he fell asleep under the lone broom bush.

Suddenly an angel shook him awake and said, "Get up and eat!"

6 He looked around and, to his surprise, right by his head were a loaf of bread baked on some coals and a jug of water. He ate the meal and went back to sleep.

7 The angel of GOD came back, shook him awake again, and said, "Get up and eat some more—you've got a long journey ahead of you."

8-9 He got up, ate and drank his fill, and set out. Nourished by that meal, he walked forty days and nights, all the way to the mountain of God, to Horeb. When he got there, he crawled into a cave and went to sleep.

Then the word of GOD came to him: "So Elijah, what are you doing here?"

[10] "I've been working my heart out for the GOD-of-the-Angel-Armies," said Elijah. "The people of Israel have abandoned your covenant, destroyed the places of worship, and murdered your prophets. I'm the only one left, and now they're trying to kill me."

[11-12] Then he was told, "Go, stand on the mountain at attention before GOD. GOD will pass by."

A hurricane wind ripped through the mountains and shattered the rocks before GOD, but GOD wasn't to be found in the wind; after the wind an earthquake, but GOD wasn't in the earthquake; and after the earthquake fire, but GOD wasn't in the fire; and after the fire a gentle and quiet whisper.

[13-14] When Elijah heard the quiet voice, he muffled his face with his great cloak, went to the mouth of the cave, and stood there. A quiet voice asked, "So Elijah, now tell me, what are you doing here?" Elijah said it again, "I've been working my heart out for GOD, the GOD-of-the-Angel-Armies, because the people of Israel have abandoned your covenant, destroyed your places of worship, and murdered your prophets. I'm the only one left, and now they're trying to kill me."

[15-18] GOD said, "Go back the way you came through the desert to Damascus. When you get there anoint Hazael; make him king over Aram. Then anoint Jehu son of Nimshi; make him king over Israel. Finally, anoint Elisha son of Shaphat from Abel Meholah to succeed you as prophet. Anyone who escapes death by Hazael will be killed by Jehu; and anyone who escapes death by Jehu will be killed by Elisha. Meanwhile, I'm preserving for myself seven thousand souls: the knees that haven't bowed to the god Baal, the mouths that haven't kissed his image."

[19] Elijah went straight out and found Elisha son of Shaphat in a field where there were twelve pairs of yoked oxen at work plowing; Elisha was in charge of the twelfth pair. Elijah went up to him and threw his cloak over him.

[20] Elisha deserted the oxen, ran after Elijah, and said, "Please! Let me kiss my father and mother good-bye—then I'll follow you."

"Go ahead," said Elijah, "but, mind you, don't forget what I've just done to you."

[21] So Elisha left; he took his yoke of oxen and butchered them. He made a fire with the plow and tackle and then boiled the meat—a true farewell meal for the family. Then he left and followed Elijah, becoming his right-hand man.

Questions for Discussion:

1. Having just experienced the extraordinary power of God on Mt. Carmel and the awesome answer to pray for rain, what do you think Elijah anticipated as he ran towards Jezreel, the nation's center of Baal worship?

2. What was Elijah's reaction to Jezebel's threat? What factors might have contributed to his reaction?

3. How did Elijah's physical overexertion affect his ability to think clearly?

4. Share situations in your experience when physical fatigue contributed to your inaccurate perception of the circumstances.

   What practical steps can you take to avoid wrong decisions influenced by physical or emotional fatigue?

5. What did Elijah do when he arrived at Horeb (1 Kings 19:9-21)?

   What was God's word to him at that time? What did God's question indicate about his opinion of Elijah's behavior?

6. How did Elijah answer the Lord?

   What attitudes did Elijah's response convey?

   When have you felt similarly to Elijah?

High demands such as work overload and personal conflicts with low control are bad enough. But combine high demand, low control with low support and the results can be disastrous. Residents face intense work demands, with limited control, work-home interference, debt, uncertain future, and relationships with other residents and faculty that may be stressful.

Preventing burnout can be addressed by increasing control, family support, and perception of effectiveness. The most important factor is the support from family and close friends about the extra work hours. Also having a quiet period of time each day to relax and reflect.

The risk can be reduced by setting realistic expectations, spending time with spouse, family and friends, and utilizing individualized approaches to reduce stress such as exercise, movies, sports, nature, or devotional time.

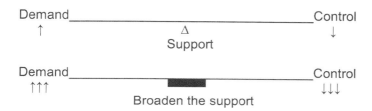

Time away does not necessarily help with burnout because it is a consequence of the work place. Burnout differs from depression in that burnout only involves a person's relationship to his or her work, whereas depression globally affects a person's life.

Some degree of burnout seems inevitable in residency. Can you think of any practical ways you can broaden your own support base? **Discuss your sense of burn out with each other and offer any suggestions or ways to better manage the situation.**

Close in prayer for one another focusing on God's goodness and his ability to protect and provide.

Elijah needed to adjust his perspective of reality. When in a similar situation of exhaustion and distorted perspective, we also need to adjust our perspective. We need God's perspective. Rest and worship will help us gain God's perspective.

If you cannot make it to a worship service in the near future, get a worship CD and worship in your car on the way to and from work. Learn the words of a simple hymn or worship song and sing to God throughout your day.

Meeting #9: Spiritual Transformation

Have you ever wished that the Holy Spirit would wave a magic wand and transform you into Christ-likeness, kind of like a super-hero? It would be instantaneous and painless!

Sometimes residency brings out the worst in us, when we are exhausted emotionally as well as physically. We find ourselves reacting to requests in ways we are not proud of. One resident described "throwing fits in my head" when one of the nurses made yet another request. The resident didn't actually say the words out loud, but she thought them . . . loudly. Some of us with less self-control and less sleep *have* said them out loud and added a little drama as well.

"For I have the desire to do what is good, but I cannot carry it out. For what I do is not the good I want to do; no, the evil I do not want to do---this I keep on doing." Romans 7: 18-19

Although the Bible does not explicitly lay out a "how to" or step by step plan of spiritual transformation, Paul's letter to the Colossians describes the process.

Instructions and Questions for Discussion:

1. Read through Colossians 3:1-17 included on the next page.

2. Go back and re-read the passage looking for clues to spiritual transformation.   Mark the phrases you would include in a "how to" manual for spiritual transformation. (Brainstorm)

3. Organize your brainstorm (into a "how to" format)

4. Note any key attitudes or essential knowledge necessary for transformation.

5. According to Colossians 3:1-17 what role does community play in the process of Christ-likeness?

6. But exactly *HOW* are we to "put off" our earthly nature and to "put on" our new self? Describe the process in your own words.

7. Consider one step you would like to take over the next couple weeks in either taking off the old self or putting on the new. Discuss how you might do this with one another.

Colossians 3: 1-17 [1]Since, then, you have been raised with Christ, set your hearts on things above, where Christ is seated at the right hand of God. [2]Set your minds on things above, not on earthly things. [3]For you died, and your life is now hidden with Christ in God. [4]When Christ, who is your life, appears, then you also will appear with him in glory. [5]Put to death, therefore, whatever belongs to your earthly nature: sexual immorality, impurity, lust, evil desires and greed, which is idolatry. [6]Because of these, the wrath of God is coming. [7]You used to walk in these ways, in the life you once lived. [8]But now you must rid yourselves of all such things as these: anger, rage, malice, slander, and filthy language from your lips. [9]Do not lie to each other, since you have taken off your old self with its practices [10]and have put on the new self, which is being renewed in knowledge in the image of its Creator. [11]Here there is no Greek or Jew, circumcised or uncircumcised, barbarian, Scythian, slave or free, but Christ is all, and is in all. [12]Therefore, as God's chosen people, holy and dearly loved, clothe yourselves with compassion, kindness, humility, gentleness and patience. [13]Bear with each other and forgive whatever grievances you may have against one another. Forgive as the Lord forgave you. [14]And over all these virtues put on love, which binds them all together in perfect unity. [15]Let the peace of Christ rule in your hearts, since as members of one body youwere called to peace. And be thankful. [16]Let the word of Christ dwell in you richly as you teach and admonish one another with all wisdom, and as you sing psalms, hymns and spiritual songs with gratitude in your hearts to God. [17]And whatever you do, whether in word or deed, do it all in the name of the Lord Jesus, giving thanks to God the Father through him.

Close in prayer: Read through the following passage and use it as the basis for your prayer as you pray for each other.

[1-2] So here's what I want you to do, God helping you: Take your everyday, ordinary life—your sleeping, eating, going-to-work, and walking-around life—and place it before God as an offering. Embracing what God does for you is the best thing you can do for him. Don't become so well-adjusted to your [*medical sub-*]culture that you fit into it without even thinking. Instead, fix your attention on God. You'll be changed from the inside out. Readily recognize what he wants from you, and quickly respond to it. Unlike the culture around you, always dragging you down to its level of immaturity, God brings the best out of you, develops well-formed maturity in you.

Romans 12:1-2 (The Message)

Dear Lord God, I pray that every day_____ would place her/his life before you as an offering. That she/he would truly see how embracing your will for her/his life is the best thing she/he can do for you. I pray that _____ would never be so at home in this culture that she/he becomes unaware of its influence on her/him. Instead may _____fix her/his attention on you. Change her/him from the inside out so that she/he may recognize what you want and respond quickly. Lord God, may _____ grow up into your likeness and may your favor rest upon her/him.

In Jesus' name and to His glory!
Amen.

Meeting #10: Trying vs. Training

Our last meeting was about spiritual transformation - - - putting off the old self and putting on the new, and just how that process actually takes place. At the end of the meeting you considered one step that you might take in the process.

Do you remember what that step was? How did it go?

The process of spiritual transformation is not a quick one with simple steps you can check off as you go. What if we don't have the luxury of time? . . . Time to spend in studying the Scriptures or in prayer? What if every time I try to have devotions, I end up sleeping?

Have you ever felt discouraged with the process, or failed at bringing about the change you hoped for?

"I have come to believe that the problem is not that we do not want to change, nor is the problem that we are not trying to change. The problem is that we are not training. We have never been taught a reliable pattern of transformation."[5]

James Bryan Smith, *The Good and Beautiful God*

Read Hebrews 12:7-11 (The Message)

God is educating you; that's why you must never drop out. He's treating you as dear children. This trouble you're in isn't punishment; it's training, the normal experience of children. Only irresponsible parents leave children to fend for themselves. Would you prefer an irresponsible God? We respect our own parents for training and not spoiling us, so why not embrace God's training so we can truly live? While we were children, our parents did what seemed best to them. But God is doing what is best for us, training us to live God's holy best. At the time, discipline isn't much fun. It always feels like it's going against the grain. Later, of course, it pays off handsomely, for it's the well-trained who find themselves mature in their relationship with God.

---

[5] James Bryan Smith, *The Good and Beautiful God: Falling in Love with the God Jesus Knows* (Downers Grove, IL: InterVarsity Press, 2009), 20.

Questions for Discussion:

1. How is God using your present situation to help you grow spirituality?

2. How does God's training sometimes feel like you are going against the grain?

   Why do you think this is?

3. What is the difference between trying and training to be like Christ?

Describe your own experience with trying to change.

Could it be that the problem was not a lack of effort, but a lack of proper training?

As students and residents you are in the midst of the training process professionally. You began this training in medical school as you studied anatomy, physiology, microbiology, pathology, and other subjects. You were trained to interview and examine patients. You practiced developing a differential diagnosis and creating a plan to diagnose using laboratory and imaging studies. You were instructed on skills for best communication and practiced negotiating a plan with patients so that they could follow through. Each level of training builds on the previous level of knowledge and skills. You do not become a physician by trying, but by training.

The process of spiritual growth is similar to the process of medical education and professional development. You have been engaged in the process long enough to realize what you thought was next to impossible a year ago has now become second nature. It was through continued study, practice, feedback, evaluation, and then more study and practice that you have achieved resident status.

A discipline is any activity that one practices in order to achieve what one cannot do by trying.[6] A spiritual discipline is a discipline designed to help change one's heart, mind, emotions, and will, to become like Christ's. When we think of spiritual disciplines we think of the traditions of Bible study, meditation, prayer, fasting, and the like. But some of these disciplines are not well suited to residency training !

Yet we KNOW that we GROW spiritually during some of the toughest times in our lives. So how can we leverage the difficult times of residency to grow spiritually???

A spiritual discipline is *any activity* designed to help change us to become more like Christ. A discipline must be practiced intentionally and with a certain level of intensity in order to be transformational. Just like lifting weights---in order to progress you must increase the weight or change up the exercises.

Example of a simple discipline to train in Christ-likeness taken from residency:

Step 1: Choosing a behavior you want to address

"It seems like lately every time I get off the phone with my mother, I feel bad that I treated her so poorly. I know she loves me and is just trying to help, but her comments do more harm than good. Then I cut her off because I'm so exhausted and we hang up. It is difficult for both of us."

The above response of an intern to her mother reveals anger and frustration, resulting in sarcasm and rudeness. The response may be partially **triggered** by exhaustion and lack of emotional support (which often are 'givens' during residency.)

Step 2: Identifying the belief behind the emotion

"My underlying belief is that she should be able to understand my schedule and the demands on my time better, and not have such unrealistic expectations. **My underlying belief is** that she should be able to help me, cheer me up, make me feel less lonely, encourage me. I'm not really angry

---

[6]Dallas Willard, *The Divine Conspiracy: Rediscovering Our Hidden Life in God* (San Francisco: Harper Collins, 1998), 353.

with her, but I'm angry about my lack of control over my life, and her suggestions to help me 'fix it' are just unrealistic. **My underlying belief is** . . . that it is all about me!"

Step 3: Comparing your underlying belief with the truth

"The truth is that it is not all about me and that no one else is responsible for my feelings and emotions except me. We all have family and/or friends to support and encourage us, but it is a mutual responsibility. I should not take my frustration and anger about my situation out on my mom. I need to turn to God first and pray about my needs and not just dump on my closest friends and family."

Step 4: Creating a discipline to address the behavior and change the habit

My routine is to call my mother on the way home after call before I go to sleep. It would be better to sleep first and then call when I'm a little rested. When I pick up the phone to call her, I will pause and ask myself, 'Is this a good time to talk? Do I need to talk to God first and tell Him all my woes, before dumping the load on my mother?' I will program God into my phone so that his name pops up first under contacts (**A**lmighty God). That will remind me if I need to talk to Him first before whoever I'm calling."

If she calls me, before I answer the call I will ask myself if I am in the right frame of mind to talk with her, and if not, I will wait and call her back after I am in a better state of mind. I think I will let her know that if I don't answer her call right away it is not because she is not a priority, but that sometimes I need to sleep first or take care of some urgent business, and then call her when I can listen better."

This example is not your traditional spiritual discipline, but it is an exercise that is designed to help change one's heart, mind, emotions, and will, to become like Christ's, and it can be carried out within the constraints of residency.

Think through your daily challenges to Christ-likeness and choose one to describe below. (poor attitude, lack of trust in God, critical spirit, cynicism . . . throwing fits in your head!) Identify a recurring situation in which you struggle to respond in a way that honors God.

Step 1: Choosing a behavior you want to address

What is **triggering** your un-Christ-like response? (Although the lack of sleep, lack of down time, and heavy work-load are all factors that contribute to our un-Christ-like responses, these are factors that we only have limited control over.)

Step 2: Identifying the belief behind the emotion

The key is identifying the **underlying belief** that is tripping you up. What are you believing when your spouse or the nurse asks you something that causes you to snap? What are you believing as you drive into work that colors your entire outlook for the day ahead? Write down the underlying belief, and then see if there is a deeper belief underlying that one!

Step 3: Comparing your underlying belief with the truth

If you can identify the deep foundational belief, then you can filter it through the Word of God to see if it is true. Replace the belief with what the Scripture says is true. What is the **truth?** Note any pertinent Scriptures.

What would be your **ideal response** in this situation?

Step 4: Creating a discipline to address the behavior and change the habit

Is there a way to imbed a **reminder** into your routine that will cause you to realign your thoughts with God's word or will? This is a soul training exercise! Help each other develop a relevant exercise to practice over the next month. My exercise to address what I want to change is:

[blank box]

This lesson just begins to touch on the idea of training vs. trying to become more like Christ. The next lesson will continue to build on this principle. Training vs. trying to be like Christ involves the work of the Holy Spirit, God's Word, and the accountability and encouragement of other Christians.

Close this lesson spending some time praying for each other and for the exercise you have each chosen to practice over the next month. Thank God for His Word, His Spirit, His Son, and each other!

Meeting #11: Transforming Our Mind

The last meeting was about **trying vs. training** and how the whole process of transformation actually occurs. We can *try* to run a marathon, but fail after a couple miles, but if we *train* to run a marathon, we will be much more likely to succeed.

So too, spiritual exercises help us train to become more like Christ so we can respond to life events and those around us as Jesus would.

At the last meeting you chose an exercise to practice over the interim. How is it going? Have you had any opportunities to implement your training exercise? What do you need to do differently to be more effective in your training for spiritual growth?

Colossians 3 describes putting off the old self and putting on the new. A significant part of this transformation process occurs as we "set our minds on things above." We can renew our minds through studying and meditating on God's word. Colossians 3:16 admonishes us to, "*Let the word of Christ dwell in you richly* as you teach and admonish one another with all wisdom, and as you sing psalms, hymns and spiritual songs with gratitude in your hearts to God." (emphasis added)

Can you think of a verse that has helped you deal with life? Perhaps you memorized it so you could quickly call it to mind at a moment's notice. Even the process of memorizing verses causes us to dwell on them. **Share a favorite verse and how it has helped you.**

Isaiah 26:3 is a good verse for residency: You will keep in perfect peace those whose minds are steadfast, because they trust in you. (TNIV)

The context of this verse is a liturgy of thanksgiving used by the people as they entered Jerusalem celebrating victory. The good news of this verse has been proven over the centuries by believers throughout the world. I thoroughly tested the truth of this verse in the first month of my intern year.

Yep, this was my NICU verse, which became my mantra with each wave of anxiety that welled up inside of me as I ran between the delivery room and the rows of beeping isolettes and hovering nurses. The good news is that verses don't wear out, they become our own. My version still goes like this: "The steadfast of mind, Thou wilt keep in perfect peace, because she trusts in Thee" (adapted from the NASB).

Colossians 3:16 says, "Let the word of Christ dwell in you richly. . ." In order for God's word to dwell in us, we must dwell on it. We must be intentional about keeping God's word in our mind, so that we become saturated in it. With all the multi-tasking, routine busyness, and media messages that come at us through every conceivable avenue, we must choose - - - We must choose to dwell on God's word, because no one else will choose it for us. It is no longer about a Sunday school competition to see who can memorize the most verses. Studying and meditating on scripture is vital to our becoming more like Christ.

Work through the following study questions, and share your insights with each other.

1. Circle key words or phrases in the following Scriptures.

    But his delight is in the law of the LORD, and on his law he meditates day and night. He is like a tree planted by streams of water, which yields its fruit in season and whose leaf does not wither. Whatever he does prospers.   Psalm 1: 2, 3 (NIV)

    Your word is a lamp to my feet and a light for my path.
                                                    Psalm 119:105 (NIV)

    The unfolding of your words gives light; it gives understanding to the simple.   Psalm 119:130 (NIV)

    Great peace have they who love your law, and nothing can make them stumble.   Psalm 119:165 (NIV)

    All scripture is inspired by God and is useful for teaching the faith and correcting error, for resetting the direction of a man's life and training him in good living. The scriptures are the comprehensive equipment of the man of God, and fit him fully for all branches of his work.   2 Timothy 3:15, 16   (J.B. Phillips)

    But be ye doers of the word, and not hearers only, deceiving your own selves.   James 1:22 (KJV)

2. What do you learn about the value of Scripture from the verses above?

3. Select a key verse from those listed above and complete the verse study below.

Verse reference:

(pick out 2 key words from the verse and then define each one in the next step)

Key word:

Definition:

Key word:

Definition:

Paraphrase the verse in your own words.

How can you apply the truth of this verse to your life today?

Scripture serves as a plumb line for our lives. A plumb line is a vertical reference line used by builders and bricklayers to ensure that their constructions are perfectly vertical or upright. A plumb-bob is a weight that is suspended from a string which is then called a plumb-line and used as a vertical reference. (Originally the weight was made from lead and so the name "plumb" bob taken from the Latin word for lead.)

As a carpenter, Jesus probably used plumb lines in his work. In the Old Testament there are references to the Lord's plumb line (2 Kings 21:13; Isaiah 28:17; Amos 7:7-8; Zechariah 4:10), which almost always measured how the people lived compared with how God had intended them to live according to His Word. Much of the work of the prophets was to warn God's people how crooked and warped they had become, regardless of how *self-*righteous they seemed in their own eyes.

> "This is what he showed me: The Lord was standing by a wall that had been built true to plumb, with a **plumb line** in his hand. [8] And the LORD asked me, "What do you see, Amos?"
>
> "A plumb line," I replied. Then the Lord said, "Look, I am setting a **plumb line** among my people Israel; I will spare them no longer."
> Amos 7:7-8

The metaphor is used again in Isaiah 28: 16-17:

[16] So this is what the Sovereign LORD says:
"See, I lay a stone in Zion,
a tested stone,
a precious cornerstone for a sure foundation;
the one who trusts will never be dismayed.

[17] I will make justice the **measuring line**
and righteousness the **plumb line**;

Jesus Christ himself is the cornerstone and he is our sure foundation. He is the living Word, the Truth. We have the written word, The Bible, to serve as a plumb line for our lives. So when we are "off" or misguided, we have a standard we can trust.

Begin to create your own plumb-line (or life line):

1. Identify needs or tendencies in your life where you are not thinking or behaving according to Scripture (crooked or warped).

2. Find verses which address your weaknesses.

3. Commit one of the verses to memory and use it when you are feeling vulnerable.

4. Gradually add to your verses creating a list of verses that empower you.

This is a prayerful process and not something to be done hastily. The usefulness of your life line will depend in part on how accurately you can identify your own vulnerabilities with the help of the Holy Spirit. This practice has been a powerful tool for many people. A list of verses to help get you started is attached to the end of this lesson.

Close in prayer. Spend some time in silent prayer asking the Holy Spirit to reveal to you an area of weakness or an area where you are believing a lie. Thank God for his Word and pray for each another. Close praying the Lord's Prayer together.

Verses to help in creating a plumb-line:

Set your **hearts** on things above, where Christ is seated at the right hand of God. Set your **minds** on things above, not on earthly things. For you died, and your life is now hidden with Christ in God.
Colossians 3:1b-2 NIV

Unhappy
. . .the joy of the Lord is your strength. Nehemiah 8:10

He heals the brokenhearted, and binds up their wounds.
Psalm 147:3 NIV

Let him have all your worries and cares, for he is always thinking about you and watching everything that concerns you.
1 Peter 5:7 LB

Fear
The Lord is my light and my salvation. Whom shall I fear? The Lord is the strength of my life; of whom shall I be afraid? Psalm 27:1

I will say of the Lord, He is my refuge and my fortress: my God; in him will I trust. Psalm 91:2

May our Lord Jesus Christ himself and God our Father, who has loved us and given us everlasting comfort and hope which we don't deserve, comfort your hearts with all comfort, and help you in every good thing you say and do. 2 Thessalonians 2:16, 17 LB

Discouragement
For I am the Lord your God, who upholds your right hand, who says to you, Do not fear, I will help you. Isaiah 41:13

When you go through deep waters and great trouble, I will be with you. When you go though rivers of difficulty, you will not drown! When you walk through the fire of oppression, you will not be burned up---the flames will not consume you. Isaiah 43:2 LB

God is our refuge and strength, a very present help in trouble.
Psalm 46:1 KJV

Each time he said, "No. But I am with you; that is all you need. My power shows up best in weak people." Now I am glad to boast about how weak I am; I am glad to be a living demonstration of Christ's power, instead of showing off my own power and abilities.
2 Corinthians 12:9 LB

O my soul, don't be discouraged. Don't be upset. Expect God to act! For I know that I shall again have plenty of reason to praise him for all that he will do. He is my help! He is my God! Psalm 42:11 LB

Cast your cares on the Lord and he will sustain you; he will never let the righteous be shaken. Psalm 55:22 NIV

These things I have spoken to you, that in me you may have peace. In the world you have tribulation, but take courage; I have overcome the world. John 16:33

Good Reputation
Listen to me, you who know the right from the wrong and cherish my laws in your hearts: don't be afraid of people's scorn or their slanderous talk. Isaiah 51:7 LB

Guidance/Direction
I will instruct you and teach you in the way which you should go. I will counsel you with my eye upon you. Psalm 32:8 NASB

He guides the humble in what is right and teaches them his way. Psalm 25:9 NIV

If I take the wings of the dawn, if I dwell in the remotest part of the sea, even there thy hand will lead me, and thy right hand will lay hold of me. Psalm 139:9, 10 NASB

Wisdom
If any of you lacks wisdom, let him ask of God, who gives to all men generously and without reproach, and it will be given to him. James 1:5 NASB

Perseverance
Do not throw away your confidence, which has a great reward. For yet a very little while, he who is coming will come and will not delay. Hebrews 10:35, 37 NASB

And let us not get tired of doing what is right, for after a while we will reap a harvest of blessing if we don't get discouraged and give up. Galations 6:9 LB

Seeking God
He is a rewarder of them that diligently seek him. Hebrews 11:6 KJV

The effective prayer of a righteous man can accomplish much. James 5:16 NASB

Feeling Inadequate
I have been crucified with Christ; and it is no longer I who live, but Christ lives in me; and the life which I now live in the flesh I live by faith in the Son of God, who loved me, and delivered himself up for me.   Galations 2:20 NASB

Let us therefore come boldly unto the throne of grace, that we may obtain mercy, and find grace to help in time of need.
                                                                        Hebrews 4:16 KJV

Resources:

Boa, Kenneth. *The Heart of God: Praying the Scriptures to Expand Your Vision.* Grand Rapids, MI: Baker Books, 2005.

Wilkerson, David. *The Jesus Person Pocket Promise Book: 800 Promises from the Word of God.* Ventura, CA: Regal Books, 1994.

Meeting #12: Creating God in Our Image

At times physicians are accused of acting like they are god. But all of us have tendencies to think that the world revolves around us. Our own perspective and understanding colors everything we do. We tend to project our human perspective on God. Instead of being transformed into his likeness, we choose to define God by our rules.

Author James Bryan Smith in *The Good and Beautiful God,* includes this diagram of spiritual transformation.[7]

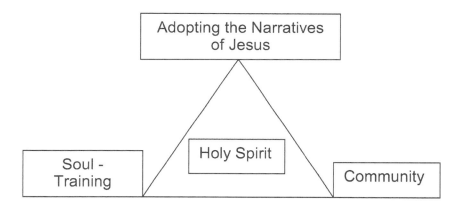

The primary means of change are the Bible and the Holy Spirit within the community of the fellow believers (2 Corinthians 3:18). Soul-training exercises are practices that help us apply the truth of Scripture to our lives. They include any activity designed to help change us to become more like Christ.

This lesson will focus on **adopting the narratives of Jesus**. We all have narratives, or stories that we live by. They serve as descriptions and explanations of how the world works, who we are, why we are the way we are, and who God is, etc. Adopting the narratives of Jesus means changing our own perspective and world view to align with Jesus' perspective. Put simply, we want to see God the way Jesus does. One way to do this is to study the parables and lessons that Jesus told about the Father and His Kingdom.

---

[7] James Bryan Smith, *The Good and Beautiful God: Falling in Love with the God Jesus Knows* (Downers Grove, IL: InterVarsity Press, 2009), 20.

Read Luke 15:11-32   The Parable of the Lost Son (The Message)

Introduction: Jesus is speaking to an audience of tax collectors and sinners. The Pharisees and teachers of the law were also present and complaining among themselves about how Jesus welcomes and even eats with sinners. In response, Jesus tells a series of three parables: the lost coin, the lost sheep, and the lost son.

Parable of the Lost Son

[11-12]Then he said, "There was once a man who had two sons. The younger said to his father, 'Father, I want right now what's coming to me.'

[12-16]"So the father divided the property between them. It wasn't long before the younger son packed his bags and left for a distant country. There, undisciplined and dissipated, he wasted everything he had. After he had gone through all his money, there was a bad famine all through that country and he began to hurt. He signed on with a citizen there who assigned him to his fields to slop the pigs. He was so hungry he would have eaten the corncobs in the pig slop, but no one would give him any.

[17-20]"That brought him to his senses. He said, 'All those farmhands working for my father sit down to three meals a day, and here I am starving to death. I'm going back to my father. I'll say to him, Father, I've sinned against God, I've sinned before you; I don't deserve to be called your son. Take me on as a hired hand.' He got right up and went home to his father.

[20-21]"When he was still a long way off, his father saw him. His heart pounding, he ran out, embraced him, and kissed him. The son started his speech: 'Father, I've sinned against God, I've sinned before you; I don't deserve to be called your son ever again.'

[22-24]"But the father wasn't listening. He was calling to the servants, 'Quick. Bring a clean set of clothes and dress him. Put the family ring on his finger and sandals on his feet. Then get a grain-fed heifer and roast it. We're going to feast! We're going to have a wonderful time! My son is here—given up for dead and now alive! Given up for lost and now found!' And they began to have a wonderful time.

[25-27]"All this time his older son was out in the field. When the day's work was done he came in. As he approached the house, he heard the music and dancing. Calling over one of the houseboys, he asked what was going on. He told him, 'Your brother came home. Your father has ordered a feast— barbecued beef!—because he has him home safe and sound.'

[28-30]"The older brother stalked off in an angry sulk and refused to join in. His father came out and tried to talk to him, but he wouldn't listen. The son said, 'Look how many years I've stayed here serving you, never giving you one

moment of grief, but have you ever thrown a party for me and my friends? Then this son of yours who has thrown away your money on whores shows up and you go all out with a feast!'

31-32"His father said, 'Son, you don't understand. You're with me all the time, and everything that is mine is yours—but this is a wonderful time, and we had to celebrate. This brother of yours was dead, and he's alive! He was lost, and he's found!'"

Questions for discussion:

1. Consider the second son and contrast his attitude before he left home with his attitude when he returned. What caused him to return?

2. What lessons do you learn about God as you consider how the father responds to his son's return?

Jesus was telling this parable (along with the parable of the lost coin, and the lost sheep) to a mixed audience. He was speaking to tax collectors and sinners, as well as Pharisees and the teachers of the law. Jesus' lesson for the Pharisees and teachers of the law is found in the role of the elder son.

3. What was the elder son's response to his brother's return? Do you think what he says is accurate?

4. Can you remember a time when you have felt similar to the elder son?

5. What is the elder son's underlying belief that is leading to his anger?

We have been raised in a culture that rewards us for our performance - - - if not as a child growing up in your home, most definitely in the culture of medical training! Our training reinforces performance-based acceptance. The accolades go to those who out perform the rest of us, yet we are all high-achievers and have learned how the system works or we would not be where we are today.

It is not just in the medical culture, but our American culture seems to be built around the narrative of working hard to earn our reward. It is almost natural then, for us to project this same principle on God. How do we win God's favor or blessing? We go to church, read the Bible, give money, and try to be good. When we read this parable of the prodigal son and get to the part of the elder brother, it bothers us. We feel a twinge of sympathy. According to our narratives, that is not how it is supposed to work. That is just not fair!

6. Compare the father's attitude toward both sons.

7. What is: a) God's part and, b) our part in spiritual restoration?

8. What were the Pharisees meant to learn from this parable?

9. What qualities of God did Jesus reveal in this parable?

This is not the only scripture passage that tells the story of God's grace being greater than our story of performance-based acceptance. Can you think of others? Name another Bible story that cuts across our sense of fairness, - - - of earning your reward.

What about the parable of the workers in the vineyard who were hired at different times throughout the day and so worked different hours. Yet at the end of the day the landowner pays them all the same ? ? ? That's not how it is supposed to work!

What about Jonah in the Old Testament? Jonah did not want the Ninevites to repent. He did not want to see God's grace poured out on the great city of Nineveh.

Jonah 4:1-3:
> But Jonah was greatly displeased and became angry. He prayed to the Lord, "O Lord, is this not what I said when I was still at home? That is why I was so quick to flee to Tarshish. I knew that you are a gracious and compassionate God, slow to anger and abounding in love, a God who relents from sending calamity. Now, O Lord, take away my life, for it is better for me to die than to live."

From Jonah's perspective that is not how it is supposed to work! Jonah's case may seem extreme, but at one time or another each of us has felt the pang of "that's not how it is supposed to work!" . . . at least not according to our understanding of the world. That is why it is so important for us to learn about God from Scripture and Jesus' perspective. God is not created in our image. We need to bring our narratives under the narratives of Scripture and allow the Holy Spirit to transform them.

God's grace is so amazing that it is hard for us to grasp it. God loves us, . . . all of us, . . . all the time.

James Bryan Smith explains, "Many people believe that God is mad at them, but for some reason he has yet to punish them fully. Such people would be more comfortable had Jesus said, 'For God was so mad at the world that he sent his Son to come down and tell them to shape up, that whosoever would shape up would have eternal life,'"[8]

Closing: Consider what would happen in your daily life if you really believed that God loves you no matter what . . . God loves you in spite of . . . God loves you regardless of. . . How would that affect your thinking, your expression, your attitude, your response?

Pray: Share prayer requests with each other and then pray together thanking God for who he is, and his amazing grace.

Consider one specific action you might practice that would be an expression of God's grace, his unconditional love, to someone else. How will you incorporate this into your routine?

---

[8] James Bryan Smith, *Good and Beautiful God*, 99.

APPENDIX

This set of twelve devotions follows the **SOAP** mnemonic used in medicine for progress notes, except in these devotions it stands for **S**cripture, **O**bservation, **A**pplication and **P**rayer. The following devotions correspond to the same topics as the Bible studies. If you are using the Bible studies on a monthly basis, the corresponding devotion may be e-mailed to the others in your group in between meetings. This helps to keep the word of God in the forefront of your thoughts. If you would like an electronic copy of these devotions please send your request to **jane.goleman@osumc.edu**

S

for Scripture

O

for Observation
What do you think God is saying to you in this scripture? Ask the Holy Spirit to teach you and reveal Jesus to you.

A

for Application
Personalize what you have read, by asking yourself how it applies to your life right now. Perhaps it is instruction, encouragement, revelation of a new promise, or corrections for a particular area of your life.

P

for Prayer
This can be as simple as asking God to help you use this scripture, or it may be a greater insight regarding what He may be revealing to you. Remember, prayer is a two way conversation, so be sure to listen to what God has to say!

July Devotion
Expectations/Evaluations/Frustrations

S: 2 Corinthians 3:4-6 (TNIV)

[4]Such confidence we have through Christ before God. [5] Not that we are competent in ourselves to claim anything for ourselves, but our competence comes from God. [6] He has made us competent as ministers of a new covenant—not of the letter but of the Spirit; for the letter kills, but the Spirit gives life.

O: In this passage Paul is speaking of qualifications for ministry.

> "It is all too easy to be overly impressed with a list of credentials and to lose sight of the fact that inward changes, not outward achievement, is what validates someone in God's eyes. Such a misplaced emphasis often follows from the need for some kind of objective standard by which to evaluate a person's competence. Competency in the ministry is something that is God-given rather than humanly culture that is oriented toward such overt signs of approval culture that is oriented toward such overt signs of approval as applause and kudos."[9]

---

[9] Linda L. Belleville. *2 Corinthians,* vol. 8, *The IVP New Testament Commentary Series* (Downers Grove, IL: InterVarsity Press, 1996) p. 92.

Competency in our society is largely determined by whether we are able "to get the job done." Ministerial competency, by contrast, issues not from self but from God, who has made us competent as ministers of a new covenant (vv. 5-6).

A: Paul was referring to the apostolic ministry of proclaiming the gospel. But our work **can** be ministry if we are working with the right attitude and aim . . .with the outcome being to glorify God and further His kingdom. As physicians many of us view our work as ministry. So we study hard to understand medicine, and work hard in caring for our patients or conducting our research. In a sense we are adding to our earthly credentials. But our aim is to use all our study and work to God's glory and to serve others. So we may accumulate credentials and awards, but in the end it is God who makes us competent to be His ambassadors.

A familiar Shaker motto is, "Hands to work, and hearts to God." The Shakers believed that God should be taken into the workplace and the excellence of their work was a part of their worship. Their furniture and crafts came to be known as "religion in wood." As we study, work, and care for patients, let us be diligent in our work, yet keeping our focus on God. We look to him for the outcome of our labor. We look to him for our approval, rather working for the accolades and applause of others.

P: Father, we praise you for the beauty of your creation. For we too are part of your creation. We marvel that you would choose to work through us. Your power and wisdom shining through such weak vessels. We are dependent on you. We humble ourselves before you this day, moving forward, working hard, in your strength to *your* glory. May your kingdom come in greater measure, in us and through us this day.

S

for Scripture

O

for Observation

What do you think God is saying to you in this scripture? Ask the Holy Spirit to teach you and reveal Jesus to you.

A

for Application

Personalize what you have read, by asking yourself how it applies to your life right now. Perhaps it is instruction, encouragement, revelation of a new promise, or corrections for a particular area of your life.

P

for Prayer

This can be as simple as asking God to help you use this scripture, or it may be a greater insight regarding what He may be revealing to you. Remember, prayer is a two way conversation, so be sure to listen to what God has to say!

August Devotion
Clarifying Your Calling

S: Ephesians 2:10

"For we are God's workmanship, created in Christ Jesus to do good works, which God prepared in advance for us to do."

O: God designed us to be his masterpiece. Created in his image, we bear his stamp or trademark. It is no surprise then, that our work should be similar to his also. It should reflect his will and his ways. Not only were we created to do good works, but God prepared the work for us ahead of time. **Life's satisfaction comes in doing the work God has prepared for us . . .** Good work- - - work that can be thought of as Kingdom work. Work that reflects the values of the Kingdom - - - where he rules and reigns. Good work that is built on being in right relationship with God, one another, and creation.   What a great sense of satisfaction we experience when we find work designed for us - - - something suited to who we are. God calls us to join in Kingdom work that furthers his purposes, his glory, and his Kingdom.

A: But what if we are struggling with our work and thinking that God couldn't possibly have called us to *this* work. Remember that God is working in us to fit us for the work he has for us. Sometimes it is about being faithful with what he has put before us *today*. Sometimes it is more about being *who* he wants us to be, rather than accomplishing something great. Pastor and author R. Kent Hughes writes in his commentary on Ephesians :

". . . whatever the task to which he has called you, you will be equipped for it as surely as a bird is capable of flight. And in doing the works he has called you to do, you will be both more and more his workmanship and more and more your true self.

All of us are God's workmanship and as such we have been given "good works" to do which were appointed before our existence. And when we do them, he gives us the necessary power and a marvelous sense of the Holy Spirit in our sails. There is nothing more beautiful than his workmanship working for him." [10]

P: Father we marvel that you not only created us but also created work for us to do. It is not as if you *need* us to work for you. Yet you have invited us and welcomed us to join in your work. We humble ourselves before you, seeking to be faithful with the tasks you have given us this day. Open our eyes to see the work that you have prepared for us, and then strengthen and empower us to be ambassadors of your mercy and grace. In Jesus' name and to his glory. Amen.

---

[10] R. Kent Hughes. *Ephesians: The Mystery of the body of Christ.* (Wheaton, IL: Crossway Books, 1990) p. 86.

S

for Scripture

O

for Observation
What do you think God is saying to you in this scripture? Ask the Holy Spirit to teach you and reveal Jesus to you.

A

for Application
Personalize what you have read, by asking yourself how it applies to your life right now. Perhaps it is instruction, encouragement, revelation of a new promise, or corrections for a particular area of your life.

P

for Prayer
This can be as simple as asking God to help you use this scripture, or it may be a greater insight regarding what He may be revealing to you. Remember, prayer is a two way conversation, so be sure to listen to what God has to say!

September Devotion
The Burden of Caring with Integrity

S: Galations 6: 9

"Let us not become weary in doing good, for at the proper time we will reap a harvest if we do not give up."

O: Have you ever become weary in doing good? Weary? How about exhausted!? It is so hard to work or care for people the way we think Jesus would want us to. Everything takes time. Listening takes time. Paying attention to the details---the seemingly small requests in caring for patients are often the more important things to them. The most difficult time to care for others with integrity, the way Jesus would want us to, is when we are tired or feeling sick ourselves. Galations encourages us to not become weary in doing good. We need that encouragement! Weariness can lead to discouragement, and the desire to give up.

A: The truth is, we all need a weekly Sabbath rest. Unfortunately our culture is moving farther and farther away from this concept. So what are we to do when our jobs or circumstances prevent us from taking a regular Sabbath rest? How do we deal with our weariness? In Matthew 11: 28, 29 Jesus says:

> "Come to me, all you who are weary and burdened, and I will give you rest. Take my yoke upon you and learn from me, for I am gentle and humble in heart, and you will find rest for your souls. For my yoke is easy and my burden is light."

Ahh, rest for your soul. Doesn't that sound wonderful? When we are weary and burdened we need to take our attention off ourselves and our weariness, and focus on Jesus. What is it that He wants us to learn from him, and why would He describe his yoke as easy and his burden as light?? In his humility Jesus only did what the Father wanted him to do. He only said what the Father wanted him to say. Perhaps we take on more than the Father has asked of us. In our humility we need to confess that we are not God, and we are not called to do it all. Sometimes our weariness is due to the stress and expectations we place on ourselves. Not wanting to disappoint anyone or let someone down, we agree to too much. We work in our own strength to accomplish our own agenda. At times, we wear our weariness as a badge of proof that we are indispensible. Putting all drama aside, most of the time, when our weariness gets the better of us, we just keep putting one foot in front of the other, trying to do the next right thing. But Jesus says, "Come to me." As we exhale and surrender our weariness to Christ, His Spirit can lift our burden and in its place leave a humble and gentle heart.

P: Oh Father, we exhale our weariness and inhale more of your Spirit. We confess that we have become full of ourselves, our agenda, and our concerns. We confess and lift our eyes to you, our Provider and Protector. In your presence we are empty, we are still. Fill our emptiness with more of your Spirit. Transform our weariness into gentleness and humility. Make a way for us. We rest in you. Amen

S

for Scripture

O

for Observation
What do you think God is saying to you in this scripture? Ask the Holy Spirit to teach you and reveal Jesus to you.

A

for Application
Personalize what you have read, by asking yourself how it applies to your life right now. Perhaps it is instruction, encouragement, revelation of a new promise, or corrections for a particular area of your life.

P

for Prayer
This can be as simple as asking God to help you use this scripture, or it may be a greater insight regarding what He may be revealing to you. Remember, prayer is a two way conversation, so be sure to listen to what God has to say!

October Devotion
Finding Meaning in the Mundane: Relentless Scut-Work

S: Proverbs 8: 34

"Blessed are those who listen to me, watching **daily** at my doors, waiting at my doorway."

O: Life is SO daily! Much of what we do in one day is just repeated in the next. Have you ever become tired of the same old same old? This Scripture from the book of Proverbs is all about wisdom. Wisdom is personified and calls out to us to listen. She exhorts us to listen, to watch, and to wait---*daily*. Here it is from The Message paraphrase:

> Blessed the man, blessed the woman, who listens to me,
> awake and ready for me each morning,
> alert and responsive as I start my day's work.

When you do a search on the word 'daily' in Scripture, here are some of the verses you find:

Praise be to the Lord, to God our Savior, who **daily** bears our burdens. (Ps 68:19)

"Whoever wants to be my disciple must deny themselves and take up their cross **daily** and follow me." (Luke 9:23)

Give us each day our **daily** bread. (Luke 11:3)

. . . and to make it your ambition to lead a quiet life: You should mind your own business and work with your hands, just as we told you, so that your **daily** life may win the respect of outsiders and so that you will not be dependent on anybody. (1 Thes 4:11-12)

But encourage one another **daily**, as long as it is called "Today," so that none of you may be hardened by sin's deceitfulness. (Hebrews 3:13)

Life IS so daily. God designed it that way and He provides for us that way. So we too, must follow in His footsteps living out our lives one day at a time and encouraging others to do the same- - - one day at a time.

A Life is lived on two levels. There is the earthly level and the heavenly level, or the daily level and the eternal level. The trick is keeping both levels in mind. The earthly level is so "in your face" that sometimes it can obscure the heavenly level. That is when the mundane day-in and day-out routines seem relentless and devoid of any real joy- - - without an end in sight. We need to be reminded to listen, watch, and wait for God's wisdom, for signs of His Kingdom breaking through in and around us each day. He is speaking and we need one ear tuned in to the eternal level as we go about our daily business. It is the eternal perspective that brings real joy and makes it possible to approach each day with a thankful heart.

P: We praise you Heavenly Father, for this day and the opportunities this day to give you thanks. We confess our self-centeredness and impatience with life itself, wishing to be done with all the details and duties, so we can get on with what is *"most important."* Remind us that you are in the details. Remind us throughout the day of your presence. Give us your perspective and enable us to complete even the seemingly mundane tasks with care and integrity. To your glory. Amen

S

for Scripture

O

for Observation

What do you think God is saying to you in this scripture? Ask the Holy Spirit to teach you and reveal Jesus to you.

A

for Application

Personalize what you have read, by asking yourself how it applies to your life right now. Perhaps it is instruction, encouragement, revelation of a new promise, or corrections for a particular area of your life.

P

for Prayer

This can be as simple as asking God to help you use this scripture, or it may be a greater insight regarding what He may be revealing to you. Remember, prayer is a two way conversation, so be sure to listen to what God has to say!

November Devotion
A Sense of Entitlement

S: 2 Kings 5:11-15

Background: Naaman was the commander of the army of the King of Aram. He was a great man in the sight of his master and highly regarded, because through him the Lord had given victory to Aram. He was a valiant soldier, but he had leprosy. He heard that there was a prophet in Israel who could cure leprosy. So he asks permission from his king to go to Israel to be healed. When he and his entourage get to the prophet Elisha's home, the prophet sends a messenger out with instructions for Naaman to go wash seven times in the Jordan in order for him to be healed.

[11] But Naaman went away angry and said, "I thought that he would surely come out to me and stand and call on the name of the LORD his God, wave his hand over the spot and cure me of my leprosy. [12] Are not Abana and Pharpar, the rivers of Damascus, better than all the waters of Israel? Couldn't I wash in them and be cleansed?" So he turned and went off in a rage.

[13] Naaman's servants went to him and said, "My father, if the prophet had told you to do some great thing, would you not have done it? How much more, then, when he tells you, 'Wash and be cleansed'!" [14] So he went down and dipped himself in the Jordan seven times, as the man of God had told him, and his flesh was restored and became clean like that of a young boy.

[15] Then Naaman and all his attendants went back to the man of God. He stood before him and said, "Now I know that there is no God in all the world except in Israel. So please accept a gift from your servant."

O: Naaman was a great man. He came with a letter of endorsement from the King of Aram, lots of gifts, horses and chariots. (It seems like everyone else in the Scriptures who had leprosy would have been banned from the community!) Yet, Naaman arrives with great fanfare, and expects fanfare in return. Elisha is not impressed by pomp and circumstance. He doesn't even bother to get up and greet his guest. Instead he sends a messenger. Naaman takes it personally and is insulted. He is entitled to better treatment! And to think he travelled all the way from Aram! Naaman almost missed God's healing because of his injured sense of entitlement.

A: When have we come close to missing God's blessing because of our sense of entitlement? Perhaps we are waiting on God to show up in a particular way- - - to manifest His Spirit in our lives the way we have seen Him do it for others. We are entitled to hear from God or sense His presence at a particular time or way because we have been walking in obedience for so long! We have been studying and working long hours for years, while others are relaxing and spending time with friends and family. What if we are missing His blessing because it comes quietly through a "nobody" rather than at a public awards ceremony with pomp and circumstance?? Don't let your sense of entitlement disqualify you from the rich rewards of simple obedience.

P: O Lord, I humble myself before you. Remind me of who I am before you. Show me where that sense of entitlement comes from. We are all equal at the foot of your cross. Remove the ugly root of arrogance and replace it with your servant heart. Help me to avoid comparing myself with others, but to follow you in obedience, trusting your best for me. For your glory and not my own. Amen.

S

for Scripture

O

for Observation

What do you think God is saying to you in this scripture? Ask the Holy Spirit to teach you and reveal Jesus to you.

A

for Application

Personalize what you have read, by asking yourself how it applies to your life right now. Perhaps it is instruction, encouragement, revelation of a new promise, or corrections for a particular area of your life.

P

for Prayer

This can be as simple as asking God to help you use this scripture, or it may be a greater insight regarding what He may be revealing to you. Remember, prayer is a two way conversation, so be sure to listen to what God has to say!

December Devotion
Connecting with God

S: Luke 10: 38-42

[38] As Jesus and his disciples were on their way, he came to a village where a woman named Martha opened her home to him. [39] She had a sister called Mary, who sat at the Lord's feet listening to what he said. [40] But Martha was distracted by all the preparations that had to be made. She came to him and asked, "Lord, don't you care that my sister has left me to do the work by myself? Tell her to help me!"

[41] "Martha, Martha," the Lord answered, "you are worried and upset about many things, [42] but few things are needed—or indeed only one. Mary has chosen what is better, and it will not be taken away from her."

O: In this familiar story, Martha is doing all the work, while Mary just sits listening to Jesus oblivious that she should be doing anything else. I'm sure Martha must have been huffing and puffing and perhaps making some noise in the kitchen, *hoping* that Mary would get the hint. I wonder why she didn't just ask Mary directly, and instead interrupted Jesus to ask him to tell Mary to help. If I were Mary, I would have been mortified in front of all the guests. Mary was simply tuned into Jesus.

A: If you or I had Jesus visiting in our home, would we be Mary or Martha? Why is sitting still and listening so hard? Why is it easier to be distracted by the urgent? Sometimes I wish that God would have made prayer more difficult,--- then maybe we would try harder. As it is, you can pray anytime, anywhere. You can pray out loud or silently, sitting down, kneeling or standing. You can pray by your self or with others. Maybe if we were only permitted to pray at a particular time and had to meet certain requirements beforehand . . . Prayer is so easy, that it is difficult. Access to God is not limited. He has made a way for us all through Jesus Christ. Prayer was the first wireless connection, and with unlimited minutes and no roaming fees. Prayer is so easy that we often put it last on our mental to-do list. It is so easy that only those who *really* want to, do.

P: Lord God, forgive us for our casual attitude towards prayer. For taking it for granted that we can talk with You whenever we want, no appointment needed. We are weak, just as your disciples were in the garden of Gethsemane. Change our hearts, strengthen our resolve to pray. Compel us to make appointments to spend time with you in prayer, because it is that important to us. In Jesus' name, Amen.

S

for Scripture

O

for Observation
What do you think God is saying to you in this scripture? Ask the Holy Spirit to teach you and reveal Jesus to you.

A

for Application
Personalize what you have read, by asking yourself how it applies to your life right now. Perhaps it is instruction, encouragement, revelation of a new promise, or corrections for a particular area of your life.

P

for Prayer
This can be as simple as asking God to help you use this scripture, or it may be a greater insight regarding what He may be revealing to you. Remember, prayer is a two way conversation, so be sure to listen to what God has to say!

January Devotion
Refusing to Take Offense

S: Genesis 50:15-21

Background: The story of Joseph (Genesis 37-50) is one of the great dramas found in the Old Testament. Joseph was his father's favorite son, which along with his youthful arrogance, laid the ground work for a ferocious sibling rivalry which ended in his being thrown into a cistern, and later sold into slavery. His life seemed to be a roller coaster of ups and downs. He repeatedly experienced unjust consequences, from being sold into slavery by his brothers, to escaping the snare of seduction by his master's wife, only to be thrown in prison based on her false accusations. In prison he interpreted a dream for Pharaoh's cupbearer only to be forgotten when the cupbearer was restored to his position. But two years later the cupbearer remembered Joseph and he was released from prison to interpret Pharaoh's dream. Pharaoh ends up putting Joseph in charge of the whole land of Egypt, and Joseph reunites with his brothers after they come to Egypt to buy food.

[15] When Joseph's brothers saw that their father was dead, they said, "What if Joseph holds a grudge against us and pays us back for all the wrongs we did to him?" [16] So they sent word to Joseph, saying, "Your father left these instructions before he died: [17] 'This is what you are to say to Joseph: I ask you to forgive your brothers the sins and the wrongs they committed in treating you so badly.' Now please forgive the sins of the servants of the God of your father." When their message came to him, Joseph wept.

[18] His brothers then came and threw themselves down before him. "We are your slaves," they said.

[19] But Joseph said to them, "Don't be afraid. Am I in the place of God? [20] **You intended to harm me, but God intended it for good** to accomplish what is now being done, the saving of many lives. [21] So then, don't be afraid. I will provide for you and your children." And he reassured them and spoke kindly to them.

O: It is easy to see God's sovereignty when looking back over Joseph's life, but what about in the midst of the action? What about from the bottom of a dry cistern . . . or while in the dark dungeon in Egypt? Joseph had a lot of time to think.

Genesis 50:20 is a favorite verse. "As for you, you meant evil against me, *but* God meant it for good . . . " (NAS). Even though Joseph had already explained to his brothers that he had forgiven them and that they should forgive themselves, because it was all according to God's plan (Genesis 45:5,8), they were not convinced. So when their father died, they concocted a plan to secure their safety.

How was Joseph able to forgive? He chose not to take offense or to get revenge. (Although he did cause his brothers a lot of grief before revealing who he really was!) How was Joseph able to gain God's perspective? I wonder how long it took him to get to the place where he could honestly say, "You meant evil against me, but God meant it for good."

A: Forgiving others the way that God forgives us, is the challenge. Gaining God's perspective is the key. It is next to impossible to gain God's perspective without first receiving His forgiveness. And how can we receive his forgiveness if we cannot see our own need for it?

At some point during Joseph's time in prison, he must have realized who he was before God. In contrast to his youthful boasts about his dreams, when Pharaoh asked him to interpret his dream, his initial response was something like, "*I* can't do it, but *God* can." Joseph had humbled himself before God. In order to follow Joseph's example of perspective and forgiveness, we must acknowledge our own sinfulness before God and place ourselves completely in God's hands. Only then can we have full confidence in his sovereignty over the events in our lives.

P: Father, we are so thankful and humbled by your forgiveness provided through your Son, Jesus Christ. Help us to see others through your eyes. Give us your perspective, for it is so different from our own. We cry out to you because we are weak and you are strong. We try to justify our acts, rather than confessing and receiving forgiveness. We try to keep track of every offense, instead of passing on the forgiveness we ourselves have received. Set us free. Release us from our own sense of self-righteousness. Let us find our life in you. In Jesus name, and for his glory. Amen.

S

for Scripture

O

for Observation
What do you think God is saying to you in this scripture? Ask the Holy Spirit to teach you and reveal Jesus to you.

A

for Application
Personalize what you have read, by asking yourself how it applies to your life right now. Perhaps it is instruction, encouragement, revelation of a new promise, or corrections for a particular area of your life.

P

for Prayer
This can be as simple as asking God to help you use this scripture, or it may be a greater insight regarding what He may be revealing to you. Remember, prayer is a two way conversation, so be sure to listen to what God has to say!

February Devotion
Burnout

S: Exodus 33:12-14

[12] Moses said to the LORD, "You have been telling me, 'Lead these people,' but you have not let me know whom you will send with me. You have said, 'I know you by name and you have found favor with me.' [13] If you are pleased with me, teach me your ways so I may know you and continue to find favor with you. Remember that this nation is your people."

[14] The LORD replied, "My Presence will go with you, and I will give you rest."

O: Moses was experiencing burnout. Burnout occurs with high demand and little control. God was asking *a lot* of Moses, and the people were out of control. When Moses went up the mountain to receive the tablets of the Ten Commandments, the people lost it and created their own god, a golden calf. So by the time Moses is headed back down the mountain, he can hear the ruckus, and soon saw the people running wild.

Moses was weary of leading such an obstinate group of people. He must have felt overwhelmed most of the time. I think he had had it. God had promised Moses that he would lead the people out of Egypt to a wonderful land where his descendants would settle and prosper. Yet *now*, God has promised to send Moses into the land, but God is not going to go with him, because God has had it with the Israelites. If God's patience was tried, we can assume Moses' patience was also. How could God expect Moses to continue to lead these people when God himself had had it!

Moses pleads with God for help in leading the people. He asks God to teach him what do to, so that he may continue in God's favor. Moses reminds God that these are *His* people. This is *His* work.

A: When feeling burned out we need to broaden our base of support. That is what Moses is trying to do. He wants help in leading the people. And he definitely wants God's support. Moses told God that if His presence was not going with them, then don't send them at all.

When overwhelmed with the demands of work and unable to control the circumstances, we are caught in the middle. This is so true of practicing medicine, especially during our intern and residency years. We need the certainty of God's presence. We are inadequate for the task. We need his wisdom, his peace, his presence---his Spirit. Nothing else will do. We also need his rest.

P: Father you have brought us to this place. You have given us this work. Yet it is just too much. Help us to sit at your feet. We empty ourselves of are need for control, our need for success, our need for - - - whatever. We need you. Most of all we need you. Pour out your Holy Spirit upon us. Flood our emptiness with your presence. Give us your rest. Deep down, through and through, for your glory alone. Amen

S

for Scripture

O

for Observation

What do you think God is saying to you in this scripture? Ask the Holy Spirit to teach you and reveal Jesus to you.

A

for Application

Personalize what you have read, by asking yourself how it applies to your life right now. Perhaps it is instruction, encouragement, revelation of a new promise, or corrections for a particular area of your life.

P

for Prayer

This can be as simple as asking God to help you use this scripture, or it may be a greater insight regarding what He may be revealing to you. Remember, prayer is a two way conversation, so be sure to listen to what God has to say!

March Devotion
Spiritual Transformation

S: 2 Corinthians 4:16-18

[16] Therefore we do not lose heart. Though outwardly we are wasting away, yet inwardly we are being renewed day by day. [17] For our light and momentary troubles are achieving for us an eternal glory that far outweighs them all. [18] So we fix our eyes not on what is seen, but on what is unseen, since what is seen is temporary, but what is unseen is eternal.

O: Paul found it necessary to remind the Corinthians not to lose heart. Paul had been persecuted and physically beaten on numerous occasions because of his ministry of the Gospel. Yet just as sure as his physical body was wasting away, his spiritual self was gaining and increasing in strength. Compared to his heavenly rewards, the troubles and afflictions he faced in this life were a mere nuisance that were here today and gone tomorrow. Paul refers to them as light and momentary, because in light of eternity, they were almost inconsequential. Yet, these troubles were not actually a *nuisance* for Paul, but were instrumental in his transformation. He described his troubles as "achieving for us an eternal glory"! Paul was able to leverage this world's troubles for glory in the next! Paul's unwavering conviction and eternal perspective began with his encounter with Christ on the road to Damascus, and only increased in strength as he lived out his faith amidst all kinds of hardship while keeping his eyes on Christ.

A: In this world, we will have trouble. (John 16:33) The Corinthians believed that adversity was inconsistent with the Spirit-filled Christian life. Sometimes we are caught in the same trap. But not Paul. Why are we surprised when we hit hard times? Why are we so easily discouraged? Because we are focusing on this world --- what we can see, and hear, and touch.

Our perspective needs a major adjustment. The truth is we are being transformed day by day, and one final day when Christ returns, our transformation will be complete. Our troubles and heartaches are producing or achieving for us the most awesome and spectacular phenomena- - - eternal glory - - - *way* out of proportion to our burdens. The key to the victorious Christian life is all in our perspective. Affliction does its job of producing glory "as long as we fix our eyes on what is unseen."[11]

P: Lord God, lift our gaze. Help us take our eyes off of our troubles, off of us. We choose YOU ! We choose to believe you and your Word. We choose to rest, to trust in your goodness and your grace. We bow before you. You are our God. Thy Kingdom come, thy will be done on earth as it is in heaven. Amen.

---

[11] Linda L. Belleville. *The IVP New Testament Commentary Series: 2 Corinthians.* ed. Grant R. Osborne (Downers Grove, IL: InterVarsity Press), 129.

S
for Scripture

O
for Observation
What do you think God is saying to you in this scripture? Ask the Holy Spirit to teach you and reveal Jesus to you.
A
for Application
Personalize what you have read, by asking yourself how it applies to your life right now. Perhaps it is instruction, encouragement, revelation of a new promise, or corrections for a particular area of your life.
P
for Prayer
This can be as simple as asking God to help you use this scripture, or it may be a greater insight regarding what He may be revealing to you. Remember, prayer is a two way conversation, so be sure to listen to what God has to say!

April Devotion
Trying vs. Training

S: I Cor 9:24-27

[24] Do you not know that in a race all the runners run, but only one gets the prize? Run in such a way as to get the prize. [25] Everyone who competes in the games goes into strict training. They do it to get a crown that will not last; but we do it to get a crown that will last for ever. [26] Therefore I do not run like someone running aimlessly; I do not fight like a boxer beating the air. [27] No, I strike a blow to my body and make it my slave so that after I have preached to others, I myself will not be disqualified for the prize.

O: Paul is using the metaphor of physical training for our spiritual training. The runner who gets the prize, isn't the one who just happens to show up the day of the race and decides to "*give it a try.*" The one who runs in order to get the prize, has been intentional about the process. He has laid out a training schedule and then kept at it one day at a time. In preparation for a race, two things are essential for winning. One is sustained effort in training, and the other is avoiding distractions from the goal or training for the goal. These distractions may be good things in themselves, but not useful at the time for winning the race.

A: As Christians our goal is to run, or live our life in faithfulness to Christ. Our goal is to win the prize of Jesus Christ himself and his words, "Well done, good and faithful servant." This is a much more serious race than the Olympics, yet we are less intentional about it. This race is not a sprint but a marathon, and it seems that even our training is part of the race. How intentional are we in following Jesus in all aspects of our life? When was the last time you reviewed your personalized training program for spiritual growth?

P: Lord, we praise you that this race is not about our salvation, for you have run that race for us. This race is about our love for you, --- glorifying you in who we are and what we do. Running this race is our gift to you. Thank you for enabling us to run and for training us. Thank you for being our personal trainer. You've got our attention. Give us ears to hear your voice and your Spirit to sustain us. In Jesus Name- Amen.

S

for Scripture

O

for Observation
What do you think God is saying to you in this scripture? Ask the Holy Spirit to teach you and reveal Jesus to you.

A

for Application
Personalize what you have read, by asking yourself how it applies to your life right now. Perhaps it is instruction, encouragement, revelation of a new promise, or corrections for a particular area of your life.

P

for Prayer
This can be as simple as asking God to help you use this scripture, or it may be a greater insight regarding what He may be revealing to you. Remember, prayer is a two way conversation, so be sure to listen to what God has to say!

May Devotion
Transforming Your Mind

S: Philippians 2:5-8

In your relationships with one another, have the same attitude of mind Christ Jesus had:

6 Who, being in very nature God,
did not consider equality with God something to be used to his own advantage;
7 rather, he made himself nothing
by taking the very nature of a servant,
being made in human likeness.
8 And being found in appearance as a human being,
he humbled himself
by becoming obedient to death —
even death on a cross!

O: Paul exhorts the Philippians to have the same attitude of mind Christ Jesus had. Then he goes on to explain just what that means. Even though Christ Jesus was God, he did not use his authority or position for his advantage. . . .or for ours. As a matter of fact he became human, but not as a king or an emperor. He came to serve humanity, not to rule. But he did not leverage his power in order to serve more people or to serve to a greater degree. He served in humility. He served by loving. That was his power - - - his love for the Father and for us. His love compelled his surrendered obedience to God. It was all to the glory of God.

A: If our desire or goal is to have a transformed mind, then the outcome of that goal is to have the mind of Christ. What does that look like? Total obedience to God in all humility. Always and in all ways to consider the needs of others before our own, and to consider God's glory above all else. Living a life controlled by a transformed mind means living a sacrificial life out of love for God and others. It is then our life is hidden with Christ in God.

Set your minds on things above, not on earthly things. For you died, and your life is now hidden with Christ in God. Col 3: 2-3

P: Lord God to transform our minds, we must die to self and to this world. And apart from you and your Spirit, we are helpless in this. We call upon you! "May the God who gives endurance and encouragement give *us* the same attitude of mind toward each other that Christ Jesus had, [6] so that with one mind and one voice *we* may glorify the God and Father of our Lord Jesus Christ." (Ro 15:5, 6) Amen

S

for Scripture

O

for Observation

What do you think God is saying to you in this scripture? Ask the Holy Spirit to teach you and reveal Jesus to you.

A

for Application

Personalize what you have read, by asking yourself how it applies to your life right now. Perhaps it is instruction, encouragement, revelation of a new promise, or corrections for a particular area of your life.

P

for Prayer

This can be as simple as asking God to help you use this scripture, or it may be a greater insight regarding what He may be revealing to you. Remember, prayer is a two way conversation, so be sure to listen to what God has to say!

June Devotion
Creating God in Our Image

S: Matthew 20: 9-12

"The workers who were hired about five in the afternoon came and each received a denarius. [10] So when those came who were hired first, they expected to receive more. But each one of them also received a denarius. [11] When they received it, they began to grumble against the landowner. [12] 'These who were hired last worked only one hour,' they said, 'and you have made them equal to us who have borne the burden of the work and the heat of the day.'

O: The parable of the workers in the vineyard is one of those stories that just grates against our sense of fairness. Certain Bible stories just don't sit well with us, and this is one of them. This is a story about the kingdom of heaven. (Mt 20:1) If we want to know God better, to capture a more accurate picture of who He is, then we need to see Him through the eyes of Jesus---who knows Him best.

In this parable the land owner hires men to work in his vineyard. The people he hires first thing in the morning agree to work for one denarius. The landowner continues to hire workers throughout the day and says he will pay them whatever is right. So at the end of the day, he starts by paying those men he hired last. And he pays them one denarius. The problem comes when he pays the men he hired first, the same amount! One denarius!

A: Grace is countercultural. Our culture tells us we must earn our reward, and so must everyone else. It just isn't right if we earn our way, and then others get a free ride---or almost free. But this parable is not about fair wages. This parable is about God's grace. God greatest gifts are given based on who God is---not the merit of the one who receives the gifts. Why is it we don't want to rejoice with those who are on the receiving end of God's grace . . . like the men who were hired last and paid first? In this world, the one who works the longest gets paid the most. But in God's economy, grace is given not based on merit, but on God's character. Grace is such a challenging concept for us, because we want to apply our rules of economics, of earning our reward, to God's amazing grace.

P: Father, teach us more about your grace. We open our hearts to you. Please let your Spirit scan our hearts and show us where we fall short. Allow us to experience your grace anew and to such a degree that we are changed into your likeness. For Your Glory. Amen

Made in the USA
Lexington, KY
25 June 2013